BOB'S BURGERS

MAD LIBS®

by Billy Merrell

PSS!
PRICE STERN SLOAN
An Imprint of Penguin Random House

PRICE STERN SLOAN
Penguin Young Readers Group
An Imprint of Penguin Random House LLC

Concept created by Roger Price & Leonard Stern

Published in 2015 by Price Stern Sloan, an imprint of Penguin Random House LLC,
345 Hudson Street, New York, New York 10014. Printed in the USA.

ISBN 978-0-8431-8294-1
1 3 5 7 9 10 8 6 4 2

MAD LIBS

INSTRUCTIONS

MAD LIBS® is a game for people who don't like games! It can be played by one, two, three, four, or forty.

• RIDICULOUSLY SIMPLE DIRECTIONS

In this tablet you will find stories containing blank spaces where words are left out. One player, the READER, selects one of these stories. The READER does not tell anyone what the story is about. Instead, he/she asks the other players, the WRITERS, to give him/her words. These words are used to fill in the blank spaces in the story.

• TO PLAY

The READER asks each WRITER in turn to call out a word—an adjective or a noun or whatever the space calls for—and uses them to fill in the blank spaces in the story. The result is a MAD LIBS® game.

When the READER then reads the completed MAD LIBS® game to the other players, they will discover that they have written a story that is fantastic, screamingly funny, shocking, silly, crazy, or just plain dumb—depending upon which words each WRITER called out.

• EXAMPLE (*Before* and *After*)

"________________ !" he said ________________
EXCLAMATION ADVERB

as he jumped into his convertible ________________ and
NOUN

drove off with his ________________ wife.
ADJECTIVE

"Ouch!" he said stupidly
EXCLAMATION ADVERB

as he jumped into his convertible cat and
NOUN

drove off with his brave wife.
ADJECTIVE

MAD LIBS®

QUICK REVIEW

In case you have forgotten what adjectives, adverbs, nouns, and verbs are, here is a quick review:

An ADJECTIVE describes something or somebody. *Lumpy*, *soft*, *ugly*, *messy*, and *short* are adjectives.

An ADVERB tells how something is done. It modifies a verb and usually ends in "ly." *Modestly*, *stupidly*, *greedily*, and *carefully* are adverbs.

A NOUN is the name of a person, place, or thing. *Sidewalk*, *umbrella*, *bridle*, *bathtub*, and *nose* are nouns.

A VERB is an action word. *Run*, *pitch*, *jump*, and *swim* are verbs. Put the verbs in past tense if the directions say PAST TENSE. *Ran*, *pitched*, *jumped*, and *swam* are verbs in the past tense.

When we ask for A PLACE, we mean any sort of place: a country or city (*Spain*, *Cleveland*) or a room (*bathroom*, *kitchen*).

An EXCLAMATION or SILLY WORD is any sort of funny sound, gasp, grunt, or outcry, like *Wow!*, *Ouch!*, *Whomp!*, *Ick!*, and *Gadzooks!*

When we ask for specific words, like a NUMBER, a COLOR, an ANIMAL, or a PART OF THE BODY, we mean a word that is one of those things, like *seven*, *blue*, *horse*, or *head*.

When we ask for a PLURAL, it means more than one. For example, *cat* pluralized is *cats*.

MAD LIBS® is fun to play with friends, but you can also play it by yourself! To begin with, DO NOT look at the story on the page below. Fill in the blanks on this page with the words called for. Then, using the words you have selected, fill in the blank spaces in the story.

Now you've created your own hilarious MAD LIBS® game!

BURGER OF THE DAY

TYPE OF FOOD ____________________

EXCLAMATION ____________________

NOUN ____________________

NUMBER ____________________

ADJECTIVE ____________________

NOUN ____________________

TYPE OF LIQUID ____________________

ANIMAL ____________________

PLURAL NOUN ____________________

NOUN ____________________

NUMBER ____________________

ADJECTIVE ____________________

PART OF THE BODY ____________________

COLOR ____________________

TYPE OF FOOD ____________________

MAD LIBS®

BURGER OF THE DAY

Tired of the same old ____________ (TYPE OF FOOD)? Try Bob's latest creation, the ____________ (EXCLAMATION) Burger. It's become the most popular item on the ____________ (NOUN)! The chef starts with a/an ____________ (NUMBER)-pound all-beef patty, seasoned with a blend of ____________ (ADJECTIVE) spices and herbs. While the burger cooks on the ____________ (NOUN), Bob prepares a secret sauce using ____________ (TYPE OF LIQUID) and ____________ (ANIMAL) gravy. He toasts the ____________ (PLURAL NOUN), and then piles them high with lettuce, tomato, and two slices of ____________ (NOUN). After flipping the meat, Bob melts ____________ (NUMBER) types of cheese on top. The ____________ (ADJECTIVE) creation always brings a tear to Bob's ____________ (PART OF THE BODY). He cuts the burger in half to reveal the patty's juicy ____________ (COLOR) center. Sometimes, he balances a/an ____________ (TYPE OF FOOD) on top, as a garnish. Delicious!

MAD LIBS® is fun to play with friends, but you can also play it by yourself! To begin with, DO NOT look at the story on the page below. Fill in the blanks on this page with the words called for. Then, using the words you have selected, fill in the blank spaces in the story.

Now you've created your own hilarious MAD LIBS® game!

GENE'S FLYER

PLURAL NOUN ____________________

PART OF THE BODY ____________________

NUMBER ____________________

PLURAL NOUN ____________________

TYPE OF FOOD ____________________

TYPE OF LIQUID ____________________

NOUN ____________________

PERSON IN ROOM ____________________

NUMBER ____________________

ADJECTIVE ____________________

VERB ENDING IN "ING" ____________________

SILLY WORD ____________________

NOUN ____________________

ADVERB ____________________

MAD LIBS

GENE'S FLYER

Attention, ____________ and gentlemen! The flyer in my
PLURAL NOUN

____________ is no ordinary coupon. Sure, it grants ____________
PART OF THE BODY NUMBER

percent off your order, but it also has powers beyond your wildest

____________! Today's customers receive a free ____________
PLURAL NOUN TYPE OF FOOD

and up to three cups of ____________! Show this ____________
TYPE OF LIQUID NOUN

inside for a chance to win our Burger of the Day: the ____________
PERSON IN ROOM

Burger! The first ____________ customers also receive a/an
NUMBER

____________ photo of the chef ____________ in the kitchen
ADJECTIVE VERB ENDING IN "ING"

this morning. (My sister took it!) Use the password ____________ and
SILLY WORD

Bob will sing "Row, Row, Row Your ____________" as ____________ as he
NOUN ADVERB

possibly can. Tell him Gene said so!

MAD LIBS® is fun to play with friends, but you can also play it by yourself! To begin with, DO NOT look at the story on the page below. Fill in the blanks on this page with the words called for. Then, using the words you have selected, fill in the blank spaces in the story.

Now you've created your own hilarious MAD LIBS® game!

GRAND OPENING

ADJECTIVE ______________________

TYPE OF FOOD (PLURAL) ______________

ADJECTIVE ______________________

ADJECTIVE ______________________

PART OF THE BODY __________________

COLOR _________________________

ADJECTIVE ______________________

TYPE OF LIQUID ___________________

PART OF THE BODY __________________

ARTICLE OF CLOTHING _______________

NOUN __________________________

VERB ENDING IN "ING" _______________

ADVERB _________________________

PLURAL NOUN _____________________

TYPE OF LIQUID ___________________

MAD LIBS

GRAND OPENING

The day Bob's Burgers held its ____________ Opening, the
ADJECTIVE

restaurant caught on fire! It all started when Bob walked in on Louise throwing ____________ in the ____________ fryer. "I'm
TYPE OF FOOD (PLURAL) / ADJECTIVE

making ____________ fries!" she said. Louise didn't seem to notice
ADJECTIVE

the look of horror on her father's ____________ or the ____________
PART OF THE BODY / COLOR

smoke filling the kitchen. "They're going to be ____________ dipped
ADJECTIVE

in ____________!" Bob quickly covered his ____________ with his
TYPE OF LIQUID / PART OF THE BODY

____________ and rushed to pull Louise out of ____________'s
ARTICLE OF CLOTHING / NOUN

way. "What have I told you about ____________ with fire,
VERB ENDING IN "ING"

Louise?" Bob asked, once the Belchers were ____________ outside
ADVERB

and the firefighters had put out the ____________. "I wasn't! I
PLURAL NOUN

was playing with ____________!" his daughter argued. "The fire
TYPE OF LIQUID

happened later."

MAD LIBS® is fun to play with friends, but you can also play it by yourself! To begin with, DO NOT look at the story on the page below. Fill in the blanks on this page with the words called for. Then, using the words you have selected, fill in the blank spaces in the story.

Now you've created your own hilarious MAD LIBS® game!

TINA'S LOVE LETTER

ADJECTIVE ________________

VERB ________________

NOUN ________________

PART OF THE BODY (PLURAL) ________________

VERB ________________

PART OF THE BODY ________________

ANIMAL ________________

TYPE OF LIQUID ________________

PART OF THE BODY ________________

A PLACE ________________

COLOR ________________

CELEBRITY ________________

ARTICLE OF CLOTHING ________________

PART OF THE BODY ________________

ADJECTIVE ________________

ADJECTIVE ________________

MAD LIBS

TINA'S LOVE LETTER

Dear Jimmy Pesto Jr.,

Words cannot explain the depth of my ____________ (ADJECTIVE) love for you! Sometimes I ____________ (VERB), staring at the ____________ (NOUN) on your chin. My ________________ (PART OF THE BODY (PLURAL)) sweat and my knees ____________ (VERB). I love watching you dance your feelings, shaking your ____________ (PART OF THE BODY) like a sweaty ____________ (ANIMAL). I love watching you wipe away ______________ (TYPE OF LIQUID) mustaches with your forearm. And the way your spit hits my ____________ (PART OF THE BODY) when you say my name! Say it, Jimmy Jr.! Sometimes I dream we're in (the) ____________ (A PLACE). I'm wearing a/an ____________ (COLOR) dress. We're there with ____________ (CELEBRITY), but you only have eyes for me. You take off your ________________ (ARTICLE OF CLOTHING) and hand it to me. I hold it close to my ____________ (PART OF THE BODY) and savor your ____________ (ADJECTIVE) scent. But then I wake up. Tell me we'll go someday!

Signed,

Your Not-So-____________ (ADJECTIVE) Admirer, Tina

MAD LIBS® is fun to play with friends, but you can also play it by yourself! To begin with, DO NOT look at the story on the page below. Fill in the blanks on this page with the words called for. Then, using the words you have selected, fill in the blank spaces in the story.

Now you've created your own hilarious MAD LIBS® game!

EULOGY FOR MOOLISSA

ADJECTIVE ______________________

VERB (PAST TENSE) ______________________

ADVERB ______________________

ANIMAL ______________________

COLOR ______________________

NOUN ______________________

ADJECTIVE ______________________

TYPE OF FOOD ______________________

ADJECTIVE ______________________

NOUN ______________________

PLURAL NOUN ______________________

A PLACE ______________________

VERB ENDING IN "ING" ______________________

ADJECTIVE ______________________

PLURAL NOUN ______________________

ADJECTIVE ______________________

MAD LIBS®

EULOGY FOR MOOLISSA

We have gathered here today to remember Moolissa, our ________________ (ADJECTIVE) friend. She died as she ________________ (VERB (PAST TENSE)): deliciously! And she will not be ________________ (ADVERB) replaced. Moolissa wasn't just a/an ________________ (ANIMAL) wearing a/an ________________ (COLOR) wig. She was a/an ________________ (NOUN)! She was a/an ________________ (ADJECTIVE) symbol for the sacrifices we make in the name of ________________ (TYPE OF FOOD)! Moolissa will be remembered for her ________________ (ADJECTIVE) beauty, her sense of ________________ (NOUN), and her many ________________ (PLURAL NOUN) throughout (the) ________________ (A PLACE). We honor her by ________________ (VERB ENDING IN "ING") today, tomorrow, and always. ________________ (ADJECTIVE), but not forgotten, Moolissa lives on in our ________________ (PLURAL NOUN). Rest in peace, our ________________ (ADJECTIVE) girl!

MAD LIBS® is fun to play with friends, but you can also play it by yourself! To begin with, DO NOT look at the story on the page below. Fill in the blanks on this page with the words called for. Then, using the words you have selected, fill in the blank spaces in the story.

Now you've created your own hilarious MAD LIBS® game!

HUGO'S HEALTH INSPECTION

TYPE OF FOOD (PLURAL) ______________

NUMBER ______________

PLURAL NOUN ______________

NOUN ______________

ADJECTIVE ______________

PLURAL NOUN ______________

ANIMAL ______________

PART OF THE BODY ______________

NOUN ______________

PART OF THE BODY (PLURAL) ______________

VERB ______________

PART OF THE BODY ______________

ARTICLE OF CLOTHING ______________

ADJECTIVE ______________

NOUN ______________

PLURAL NOUN ______________

VERB ENDING IN "ING" ______________

MAD LIBS®

HUGO'S HEALTH INSPECTION

***Food Safety Checklist*:**

- Does Bob store ________________ below __________ degrees?
  TYPE OF FOOD (PLURAL) NUMBER
- Does he store ________________ at least six inches off the ________________?
  PLURAL NOUN NOUN
- Are all surfaces ________________?
  ADJECTIVE
- Are there ________________, or other evidence of ________________ infestation?
  PLURAL NOUN ANIMAL
- Does Bob wear a/an ________________ -net?
  PART OF THE BODY
- Chew ________________?
  NOUN
- Does Bob correctly wash his ________________? ________________ his nails?
  PART OF THE BODY (PLURAL) VERB
- Does he cover his ________________ when he sneezes?
  PART OF THE BODY
- Does his ________________ look ________________?
  ARTICLE OF CLOTHING ADJECTIVE
- Is he wearing more than one ________________ on his wrist?
  NOUN
- Does Bob have any open ________________ or bandages that might fall off while ________________?
  PLURAL NOUN VERB ENDING IN "ING"

MAD LIBS® is fun to play with friends, but you can also play it by yourself! To begin with, DO NOT look at the story on the page below. Fill in the blanks on this page with the words called for. Then, using the words you have selected, fill in the blank spaces in the story.

Now you've created your own hilarious MAD LIBS® game!

GRAND RE-OPENING

ADJECTIVE ____________________

ANIMAL (PLURAL) ____________________

ADJECTIVE ____________________

TYPE OF FOOD ____________________

ARTICLE OF CLOTHING ____________________

ADJECTIVE ____________________

ADJECTIVE ____________________

NUMBER ____________________

ADJECTIVE ____________________

A PLACE ____________________

PLURAL NOUN ____________________

VERB ENDING IN "ING" ____________________

PLURAL NOUN ____________________

COLOR ____________________

PART OF THE BODY (PLURAL) ____________________

ADJECTIVE ____________________

MAD LIBS®

GRAND RE-OPENING

The day of Bob's Burgers' ____________ (ADJECTIVE) Re-Opening, the restaurant became infested with ______________ (ANIMAL (PLURAL))! The night before, Gene had come up with the ____________ (ADJECTIVE) idea of making a/an ____________ (TYPE OF FOOD) costume. The only problem was, he decided to make it out of a/an ____________________ (ARTICLE OF CLOTHING) and ____________ (ADJECTIVE) meat. "What's that smell?" Linda asked Bob the next morning. But Bob couldn't smell anything. He had been ____________ (ADJECTIVE) with a cold for __________ (NUMBER) days. "Seriously, Bob. What is that? It smells ____________ (ADJECTIVE)! Actually, it reminds me of that hotel you like near (the) ____________ (A PLACE)." But when Linda saw the ______________ (PLURAL NOUN) of Gene's labor, she started dry-______________ (VERB ENDING IN "ING"). The costume had come apart at the ______________ (PLURAL NOUN)! The pile of meat had turned ____________ (COLOR) and was swarming with insects. "Is that a mouse that just ran between your ____________________ (PART OF THE BODY (PLURAL))?!" Bob yelled. But it was worse than he feared. Whatever it was, it was far too ____________ (ADJECTIVE) to be a mouse.

MAD LIBS® is fun to play with friends, but you can also play it by yourself! To begin with, DO NOT look at the story on the page below. Fill in the blanks on this page with the words called for. Then, using the words you have selected, fill in the blank spaces in the story.

Now you've created your own hilarious MAD LIBS® game!

HEY, BOO BOO

ADJECTIVE ______________________

ADJECTIVE ______________________

VEHICLE ______________________

A PLACE ______________________

ARTICLE OF CLOTHING (PLURAL) ______________________

ANIMAL ______________________

NOUN ______________________

SILLY WORD ______________________

PART OF THE BODY ______________________

ADVERB ______________________

PART OF THE BODY ______________________

MAD LIBS®

HEY, BOO BOO

A/An ____________ *letter to Boo Boo from the boy band Boyz 4 Now:*
ADJECTIVE

Dear Boo Boo

(What kind of ____________ name is that, anyway?),
ADJECTIVE

I doubt you remember me. My name is Louise. I snuck onto your tour ____________ after your concert in (the) ____________. I hid in a hamper, covered in ____________, and surprised you. I was wearing pink ____________ ears. Does any of this ring a/an ____________? Now I catch myself mumbling ____________ when I see your ____________ on my sister's wall. And it makes me sick. What should I do?

VEHICLE / A PLACE / ARTICLE OF CLOTHING (PLURAL) / ANIMAL / NOUN / SILLY WORD / PART OF THE BODY

Yours truly, ____________, deeply,
ADVERB

Louise Belcher

P.S. How's that beautiful, hideous ____________ of yours?
PART OF THE BODY

MAD LIBS® is fun to play with friends, but you can also play it by yourself! To begin with, DO NOT look at the story on the page below. Fill in the blanks on this page with the words called for. Then, using the words you have selected, fill in the blank spaces in the story.

Now you've created your own hilarious MAD LIBS® game!

ATTENTION: FRAGILE!

ADJECTIVE ______________________

PLURAL NOUN ______________________

NUMBER ______________________

VERB ______________________

VERB ______________________

NOUN ______________________

ADJECTIVE ______________________

ARTICLE OF CLOTHING ______________________

NOUN ______________________

ADJECTIVE ______________________

ADVERB ______________________

VERB ______________________

ADVERB ______________________

PLURAL NOUN ______________________

MAD LIBS

ATTENTION: FRAGILE!

Here are Linda's instructions for handling her collection of porcelain babies:

- Use ____________ (ADJECTIVE) care when holding my precious ____________ (PLURAL NOUN)!
- Only pick up ____________ (NUMBER) at a time!
- ____________ (VERB) when holding a baby! Never run!
- At night, ____________ (VERB) each little guy in his own sheet of ____________ (NOUN).
- Each ____________ (ADJECTIVE) lady gets her own ____________ (ARTICLE OF CLOTHING), made of ____________ (NOUN). (Don't they look ____________ (ADJECTIVE)?)
- Set them ____________ (ADVERB) in the box! Careful not to ____________ (VERB) them, as they'll wake up.
- They like it when you talk to them and kiss them ____________ (ADVERB) on their glazed foreheads. (All ____________ (PLURAL NOUN) need love!)

MAD LIBS® is fun to play with friends, but you can also play it by yourself! To begin with, DO NOT look at the story on the page below. Fill in the blanks on this page with the words called for. Then, using the words you have selected, fill in the blank spaces in the story.

Now you've created your own hilarious MAD LIBS® game!

BOB'S FAVORITE HOLIDAY

ADJECTIVE ________________

TYPE OF FOOD ________________

ANIMAL ________________

PERSON IN ROOM ________________

ADJECTIVE ________________

PART OF THE BODY (PLURAL) ________________

A PLACE ________________

ADJECTIVE ________________

NOUN ________________

VERB ENDING IN "ING" ________________

TYPE OF LIQUID ________________

ADJECTIVE ________________

SILLY WORD ________________

TYPE OF FOOD ________________

MAD LIBS

BOB'S FAVORITE HOLIDAY

Bob loves family traditions, especially on Thanksgiving. Bob knows he has a lot to be ______________ (ADJECTIVE) for. He gets emotional about ______________ (TYPE OF FOOD). He even names the ______________ (ANIMAL)! (Last year, he called it ______________ (PERSON IN ROOM).) Bob also gets ______________ (ADJECTIVE) about his kids. He bonds with Gene. He lays out the turkey's ______________ (PART OF THE BODY (PLURAL)) and plays *CSI*: (the) ______________ (A PLACE) with Louise. Bob spends the whole day preparing a/an ______________ (ADJECTIVE) meal for his family. He looks forward to snapping the ______________ (NOUN)-bone with Tina, and he isn't bothered by Linda's day-long ______________ (VERB ENDING IN "ING"). Or by Louise and Gene sneaking sips of ______________ (TYPE OF LIQUID). He even laughs at Tina's ______________ (ADJECTIVE) jokes. When it's finally time for his toast, Bob says only "______________ (SILLY WORD)" before Linda interrupts, singing "Pass the ______________ (TYPE OF FOOD)!"

MAD LIBS® is fun to play with friends, but you can also play it by yourself! To begin with, DO NOT look at the story on the page below. Fill in the blanks on this page with the words called for. Then, using the words you have selected, fill in the blank spaces in the story.

Now you've created your own hilarious MAD LIBS® game!

JIMMY PESTO SURVIVAL KIT

COLOR ______________________

PART OF THE BODY ______________________

SAME PART OF THE BODY ______________________

TYPE OF FOOD ______________________

PART OF THE BODY ______________________

OCCUPATION ______________________

VERB ENDING IN "ING" ______________________

PLURAL NOUN ______________________

PERSON IN ROOM ______________________

PERSON IN ROOM ______________________

ANIMAL ______________________

SAME ANIMAL ______________________

ADJECTIVE ______________________

ARTICLE OF CLOTHING ______________________

COLOR ______________________

MAD LIBS®

JIMMY PESTO SURVIVAL KIT

When challenged by his business rival, Bob follows the ____________ (COLOR) Rule: a/an ____________ (PART OF THE BODY) for a/an ____________ (SAME PART OF THE BODY). He keeps the following on hand, just in case:

- Aspirin—for Jimmy's ____________ (TYPE OF FOOD)-induced ____________ (PART OF THE BODY)-aches
- A/An ____________ (OCCUPATION) disguise—for ____________ (VERB ENDING IN "ING") into the pizzeria unnoticed
- Two matching ____________ (PLURAL NOUN)—for bribing Pesto's twins, ____________ (PERSON IN ROOM) and ____________ (PERSON IN ROOM)
- A toy ____________ (ANIMAL)—for planting in Pesto's restaurant to deter customers (a real ____________ (SAME ANIMAL) might work, too, if ____________ (ADJECTIVE))
- Photos of Jimmy with his ____________ (ARTICLE OF CLOTHING) off—to ____________ (COLOR)-mail him, if necessary

MAD LIBS® is fun to play with friends, but you can also play it by yourself! To begin with, DO NOT look at the story on the page below. Fill in the blanks on this page with the words called for. Then, using the words you have selected, fill in the blank spaces in the story.

Now you've created your own hilarious MAD LIBS® game!

GRAND RE-RE-OPENING

PERSON IN ROOM ____________________

ADJECTIVE ____________________

FIRST NAME ____________________

NOUN ____________________

VERB (PAST TENSE) ____________________

TYPE OF FOOD ____________________

ADVERB ____________________

PLURAL NOUN ____________________

ADJECTIVE ____________________

NOUN ____________________

PART OF THE BODY ____________________

NUMBER ____________________

NOUN ____________________

ADJECTIVE ____________________

PLURAL NOUN ____________________

PLURAL NOUN ____________________

MAD LIBS®

GRAND RE-RE-OPENING

The night before ______________ (PERSON IN ROOM)'s Burgers' ______________ (ADJECTIVE) Re-Re-Opening, Hurricane ______________ (FIRST NAME) blew through town, leaving a/an ______________ (NOUN) of destruction behind it. The sign for the Wonder Wharf ______________ (VERB (PAST TENSE)) down Ocean Avenue, blocking the door to Jimmy ______________ (TYPE OF FOOD)'s Pizzeria so that no one could enter. ______________ (ADVERB), none of the other ______________ (PLURAL NOUN) on the street were harmed. "Maybe it's our ______________ (ADJECTIVE) day," Bob told Linda in the morning, after the storm had ended. "We'll be the only ______________ (NOUN) on the block open today!" But no sooner had the words left his ______________ (PART OF THE BODY) than a/an ______________ (NUMBER)-foot-tall ______________ (NOUN) hit the building with a/an ______________ (ADJECTIVE) crash. ______________ (PLURAL NOUN) flew, and all of the ______________ (PLURAL NOUN) went out in the restaurant.

MAD LIBS® is fun to play with friends, but you can also play it by yourself! To begin with, DO NOT look at the story on the page below. Fill in the blanks on this page with the words called for. Then, using the words you have selected, fill in the blank spaces in the story.

Now you've created your own hilarious MAD LIBS® game!

SHADES OF YAY!

PART OF THE BODY ______________________

PART OF THE BODY ______________________

ADJECTIVE ______________________

ADJECTIVE ______________________

NOUN ______________________

PART OF THE BODY (PLURAL) ______________________

SAME PART OF THE BODY ______________________

ANIMAL ______________________

VERB ______________________

COLOR ______________________

ADJECTIVE ______________________

COLOR ______________________

A PLACE ______________________

PART OF THE BODY ______________________

NUMBER ______________________

MAD LIBS®

SHADES OF YAY!

From ____________ -shadow to ____________ -stick, no one knows
PART OF THE BODY / PART OF THE BODY

how to apply makeup better than Tammy Larson. Here are a few of her

____________ tips!
ADJECTIVE

- Make sure your face is ____________ and dry, to start.
  ADJECTIVE
- Look straight into the ____________ and apply evenly.
  NOUN
- Suck in your ____________ when you apply blush to
  PART OF THE BODY (PLURAL)
  your ____________ -bones.
  SAME PART OF THE BODY
- Then, puff your cheeks out like a/an ____________ and
  ANIMAL
  ____________ some powder on.
  VERB
- Remember: Good girls wear ____________ lipstick and
  COLOR
  ____________ girls wear ____________.
  ADJECTIVE / COLOR
- Never leave (the) ____________ without tissues and a/an
  A PLACE
  ____________ -lash curler.
  PART OF THE BODY
- And be sure to reapply every ____________ hours. At least!
  NUMBER

MAD LIBS® is fun to play with friends, but you can also play it by yourself! To begin with, DO NOT look at the story on the page below. Fill in the blanks on this page with the words called for. Then, using the words you have selected, fill in the blank spaces in the story.

Now you've created your own hilarious MAD LIBS® game!

GAYLE'S NEW PAINTINGS

NOUN ______________________

NUMBER ______________________

COLOR ______________________

A PLACE ______________________

PLURAL NOUN ______________________

ANIMAL ______________________

PART OF THE BODY ______________________

PLURAL NOUN ______________________

ADJECTIVE ______________________

CELEBRITY (MALE) ______________________

VERB ENDING IN "ING" ______________________

EXCLAMATION ______________________

ADJECTIVE ______________________

ADJECTIVE ______________________

MAD LIBS®

GAYLE'S NEW PAINTINGS

Interviewer: When did you first know you were a/an ______________ (NOUN)?

Gayle: When I was ____________ (NUMBER), I started eating my sister Linda's lipstick. I wanted to feel ______________ (COLOR) inside!

Interviewer: You recently exhibited your paintings in (the) ______________ (A PLACE). What was that like?

Gayle: Like all the great ______________________ (PLURAL NOUN), I was *censored*! I guess some people can't take the sight of a/an ______________ (ANIMAL)'s ______________ (PART OF THE BODY).

Interviewer: And your newest __________________ (PLURAL NOUN)? Can you describe them?

Gayle: I have always loved ______________ (ADJECTIVE) cats. And ______________ (CELEBRITY (MALE)). By ____________________ (VERB ENDING IN "ING"), I have united my two passions. I call the series ________________ (EXCLAMATION) Meow!

Interviewer: Simply ______________ (ADJECTIVE)!

Gayle: Thank you. But don't touch! The canvas is still ______________ (ADJECTIVE).

MAD LIBS® is fun to play with friends, but you can also play it by yourself! To begin with, DO NOT look at the story on the page below. Fill in the blanks on this page with the words called for. Then, using the words you have selected, fill in the blank spaces in the story.

Now you've created your own hilarious MAD LIBS® game!

MORT'S SECRET

TYPE OF FOOD ______________________

CELEBRITY (MALE) ______________________

PERSON IN ROOM (FEMALE) ______________________

COLOR ______________________

CELEBRITY (LAST NAME) ______________________

NUMBER ______________________

LETTER OF THE ALPHABET ______________________

NOUN ______________________

ARTICLE OF CLOTHING ______________________

PERSON IN ROOM (MALE) ______________________

CELEBRITY (FEMALE) ______________________

MAD LIBS®

MORT'S SECRET

While delivering ____________ to Mort's Funeral Home, Linda spots
TYPE OF FOOD

____________ and ________________, both wearing all
CELEBRITY (MALE) PERSON IN ROOM (FEMALE)

____________. Mort tells Linda about a secret funeral for someone
COLOR

in the ________________ family. ____________ other
CELEBRITY (LAST NAME) NUMBER

________________-list celebrities will be in attendance as well. "We
LETTER OF THE ALPHABET

have to go!" Linda tells Bob, back at the restaurant. "We're not crashing

a/an ____________, Linda!" Bob says. But Linda is already talking
NOUN

about the ________________ she intends to wear that night. When
ARTICLE OF CLOTHING

the Belchers arrive at Mort's later that evening, ________________
PERSON IN ROOM (MALE)

mistakes Linda for ____________ and insists that she sit in the
CELEBRITY (FEMALE)

front row. Linda is forced to face forward and pretend to mourn for the

rest of the ceremony. By the end she's exhausted and sad and just wants

to go home, get a box of crackers, and crawl into bed.

MAD LIBS® is fun to play with friends, but you can also play it by yourself! To begin with, DO NOT look at the story on the page below. Fill in the blanks on this page with the words called for. Then, using the words you have selected, fill in the blank spaces in the story.

Now you've created your own hilarious MAD LIBS® game!

GRAND RE-RE-RE-OPENING

ADJECTIVE ____________

NOUN ____________

VERB (PAST TENSE) ____________

PLURAL NOUN ____________

ADVERB ____________

NOUN ____________

NOUN ____________

PERSON IN ROOM ____________

NUMBER ____________

NOUN ____________

VERB (PAST TENSE) ____________

NOUN ____________

EXCLAMATION ____________

CELEBRITY (FEMALE) ____________

PLURAL NOUN ____________

NUMBER ____________

PLURAL NOUN ____________

GRAND RE-RE-RE-OPENING

The night before the ______________ (ADJECTIVE) Re-Re-Re-Opening, Bob went to sleep worried the whole ______________ (NOUN) was out to get him. He tossed and ______________ (VERB (PAST TENSE)) into the night, imagining worst-case ______________ (PLURAL NOUN) for the restaurant. When he ______________ (ADVERB) fell asleep, Bob had a nightmare. Louise and Tina had erased the ______________ (NOUN) of the Day from the chalkboard and were playing Hang-______________ (NOUN). Linda was talking on the phone with ______________ (PERSON IN ROOM), who was demanding ______________ (NUMBER) dollars of rent on behalf of Mr. Fischoeder. Then a/an ______________ (NOUN) fell out of the sky! It ______________ (VERB (PAST TENSE)) through the front ______________ (NOUN) of the restaurant! Gene cried, "______________ (EXCLAMATION)!" To everyone's horror, ______________ (CELEBRITY (FEMALE)) had been crushed! But it was only a nightmare. The next day, the opening of Bob's ______________ (PLURAL NOUN) went without a hitch. The Belchers only had ______________ (NUMBER) customers, but Bob still managed to keep the ______________ (PLURAL NOUN) open the whole day.

MAD LIBS® is fun to play with friends, but you can also play it by yourself! To begin with, DO NOT look at the story on the page below. Fill in the blanks on this page with the words called for. Then, using the words you have selected, fill in the blank spaces in the story.

Now you've created your own hilarious MAD LIBS® game!

TEDDY'S SHRINK

ADJECTIVE ______________________

TYPE OF FOOD ______________________

PART OF THE BODY ______________________

NOUN ______________________

ADJECTIVE ______________________

PART OF THE BODY (PLURAL) ______________________

VERB ______________________

VERB ENDING IN "ING" ______________________

VERB ENDING IN "ING" ______________________

ARTICLE OF CLOTHING ______________________

ADJECTIVE ______________________

ADJECTIVE ______________________

A PLACE ______________________

ADJECTIVE ______________________

ADJECTIVE ______________________

NOUN ______________________

MAD LIBS

TEDDY'S SHRINK

Therapist: Are you feeling ______________?
ADJECTIVE

Teddy: Bobby had me dress up like a/an ______________ again. My
TYPE OF FOOD
______________ broke out in hives.
PART OF THE BODY

Therapist: What is it about ______________ costumes that you find so
NOUN
______________?
ADJECTIVE

Teddy: Their soulless ______________________! I ______________
PART OF THE BODY (PLURAL) VERB
when they look at me.

Therapist: What about when *you* wear the costume? Who is
______________________ at you then?
VERB ENDING IN "ING"

Teddy (______________________ tearfully): Bobby could see my
VERB ENDING IN "ING"
______________________ sticking out. I was so ______________!
ARTICLE OF CLOTHING ADJECTIVE

Therapist: I see. And did you go to your "______________ place"? Did
ADJECTIVE
you picture yourself in (the) ______________?
A PLACE

Teddy: Yes, and it was ______________. What do you think it means?!
ADJECTIVE

Therapist: I'm ______________, but we're out of time. Let's pick up
ADJECTIVE
there next ______________.
NOUN

MAD LIBS® is fun to play with friends, but you can also play it by yourself! To begin with, DO NOT look at the story on the page below. Fill in the blanks on this page with the words called for. Then, using the words you have selected, fill in the blank spaces in the story.

Now you've created your own hilarious MAD LIBS® game!

PERSONALITY QUIZ

COLOR ____________________

ADJECTIVE ____________________

ADVERB ____________________

ADJECTIVE ____________________

ANIMAL ____________________

NOUN ____________________

TYPE OF LIQUID ____________________

NOUN ____________________

ANIMAL ____________________

ADJECTIVE ____________________

NOUN ____________________

ADJECTIVE ____________________

NOUN ____________________

MAD LIBS

PERSONALITY QUIZ

1. How do you like your burger cooked?

    a) Rare (____________ in the center)
    COLOR

    b) Medium (or ____________ to the touch)
    ADJECTIVE

    c) ____________ done (cooked all the way through)
    ADVERB

2. What is your favorite cheese?

    a) Bleu cheese (the ____________, moldy kind)
    ADJECTIVE

    b) Cheddar (or any standard ____________ cheese)
    ANIMAL

    c) No cheese for me (I'm ____________-intolerant)
    NOUN

3. Which is your favorite condiment?

    a) Dijon ____________
    TYPE OF LIQUID

    b) ____________-made mayonnaise
    NOUN

    c) ____________-sup
    ANIMAL

If you chose As, you're adventurous and ____________ (ADJECTIVE). If you chose Bs, you're a center-of-the- ____________ (NOUN) kind of person. If you chose Cs, you're cautious, predictable, and ____________ (ADJECTIVE)-to-a-fault. And if you don't eat burgers, then you're in the wrong ____________ (NOUN).

MAD LIBS® is fun to play with friends, but you can also play it by yourself! To begin with, DO NOT look at the story on the page below. Fill in the blanks on this page with the words called for. Then, using the words you have selected, fill in the blank spaces in the story.

Now you've created your own hilarious MAD LIBS® game!

JOB INTERVIEW

PERSON IN ROOM ____________________

ADJECTIVE ____________________

VERB ____________________

NUMBER ____________________

NOUN ____________________

PLURAL NOUN ____________________

ADJECTIVE ____________________

ADJECTIVE ____________________

PART OF THE BODY ____________________

ADJECTIVE ____________________

PLURAL NOUN ____________________

NUMBER ____________________

OCCUPATION ____________________

NOUN ____________________

NOUN ____________________

EXCLAMATION ____________________

VERB ENDING IN "ING" ____________________

MAD LIBS

JOB INTERVIEW

Linda: Why should we hire you, ________________?
PERSON IN ROOM

Interviewee: I'm a/an ______________ learner. I'll ______________ hard.
ADJECTIVE / VERB

I'll show up ____________ minutes early and won't leave until I get the
NUMBER

______________ done.
NOUN

Linda: What are your ________________ and weaknesses?
PLURAL NOUN

Interviewee: I don't sweat the ______________ stuff, which is both good
ADJECTIVE

and ______________. I try to keep my ________________ on the
ADJECTIVE / PART OF THE BODY

______________ picture. But I try not to let myself cut ______________,
ADJECTIVE / PLURAL NOUN

either.

Linda: Where do you see yourself in ____________ years? When I was
NUMBER

your age, I wanted to be a/an ______________ or a/an ______________
OCCUPATION / NOUN

singer!

Interviewee: I have wanted to be a chef since I was a/an ______________.
NOUN

Linda: ______________! You're hired! But don't tell Bobby that, or he
EXCLAMATION

might think I'm ________________ him out of the business.
VERB ENDING IN "ING"

Seriously, don't tell him.

MAD LIBS® is fun to play with friends, but you can also play it by yourself! To begin with, DO NOT look at the story on the page below. Fill in the blanks on this page with the words called for. Then, using the words you have selected, fill in the blank spaces in the story.

Now you've created your own hilarious MAD LIBS® game!

BURGER-EATING CONTEST

VERB ENDING IN "ING" ____________________

ADJECTIVE ____________________

TYPE OF FOOD (PLURAL) ____________________

NUMBER ____________________

PART OF THE BODY ____________________

NOUN ____________________

ADVERB ____________________

VERB ____________________

PART OF THE BODY ____________________

TYPE OF LIQUID ____________________

VERB ENDING IN "ING" ____________________

ADJECTIVE ____________________

VERB ENDING IN "ING" ____________________

PLURAL NOUN ____________________

MAD LIBS®

BURGER-EATING CONTEST

Here are Gene's tips for competitive ________________.
VERB ENDING IN "ING"

Do:

1. Know your food! There are ____________ differences between
   ADJECTIVE
   speed-eating hot dogs versus ________________.
   TYPE OF FOOD (PLURAL)
2. If the contest is __________ minutes or more, you should train
   NUMBER
   your ____________ to hold more food.
   PART OF THE BODY
3. Time yourself using a/an ____________. Practice to see how
   NOUN
   ____________ you can eat something, and then try to
   ADVERB
   ____________ your own record.
   VERB

Don't:

1. Don't put too much in your ____________ at once.
   PART OF THE BODY
2. Don't forget liquids! Have a cup of ______________ in reach. It
   TYPE OF LIQUID
   helps to moisten food and makes ________________ easier.
   VERB ENDING IN "ING"
3. Don't make yourself ____________. There's nothing worse than
   ADJECTIVE
   ________________ all over yourself in front of your
   VERB ENDING IN "ING"
   ______________ and family. Trust me! I know!
   PLURAL NOUN

MAD LIBS® is fun to play with friends, but you can also play it by yourself! To begin with, DO NOT look at the story on the page below. Fill in the blanks on this page with the words called for. Then, using the words you have selected, fill in the blank spaces in the story.

Now you've created your own hilarious MAD LIBS® game!

BOB'S THANK-YOU

PLURAL NOUN ______________________

NOUN ______________________

ADJECTIVE ______________________

TYPE OF FOOD ______________________

NUMBER ______________________

VERB ENDING IN "ING" ______________________

VERB (PAST TENSE) ______________________

ADJECTIVE ______________________

PERSON IN ROOM ______________________

ADJECTIVE ______________________

A PLACE ______________________

PART OF THE BODY ______________________

ADJECTIVE ______________________

NOUN ______________________

NOUN ______________________

PLURAL NOUN ______________________

MAD LIBS

BOB'S THANK-YOU

You ______________ are the best family a/an ______________ like me
PLURAL NOUN / NOUN

could ask for. As you know, business hasn't always been ______________.
ADJECTIVE

There are times when the last thing I want to do is make a/an ______________. And yet, I do. You ______________ are the reason I keep
TYPE OF FOOD / NUMBER

______________. Linda, you've always ______________
VERB ENDING IN "ING" / VERB (PAST TENSE)

by me, and I couldn't be more ______________. Tina, Gene, and
ADJECTIVE

______________, you make me feel like the most ______________
PERSON IN ROOM / ADJECTIVE

father in (the) ______________. From the bottom of my ______________,
A PLACE / PART OF THE BODY

thank you for all of your ______________ work, day in, ______________
ADJECTIVE / NOUN

out. Bob's Burgers wouldn't be the ______________ it is without you
NOUN

______________.
PLURAL NOUN